fingerfoods

and antipasto

TRIDENT
PRESS
INTERNATIONAL

acknowledge

Published by:
TRIDENT PRESS INTERNATIONAL
801, 12th Avenue South
Suite 302
Naples, FL 34102 U.S.A.
Copyright (c)Trident Press International 2001
Tel: (941) 649 7077
Fax: (941) 649 5832
Email: tridentpress@worldnet.att.net
Website: www.trident-international.com

Fingerfoods and Antipasto

Compiled by: R&R Publications Marketing Pty. Ltd.
Creative Director: Paul Sims
Production Manager: Anthony Carroll
Food Photography: Warren Webb, William Meppem,
Andrew Elton, Quentin Bacon, Gary Smith, Per Ericson,
Paul Grater, Ray Joice, John Stewart, Ashley Mackevicius,
Harm Mol, Yanto Noerianto, Andy Payne.
Food Stylists: Stephane Souvlis, Janet Lodge, Di Kirby,
Wendy Berecry, Belinda Clayton, Rosemary De Santis,
Carolyn Fienberg, Jacqui Hing, Michelle Gorry,
Christine Sheppard, Donna Hay.
Recipe Development: Ellen Argyriou, Sheryle Eastwood,
Kim Freeman,
Lucy Kelly, Donna Hay, Anneka Mitchell, Penelope Peel,
Jody Vassallo, Belinda Warn, Loukie Werle.
Proof Reader: Andrea Tarttelin

Includes Index
ISBN 1582791406
EAN 9781582791401

First Edition Printed June 2001
Computer Typeset in Humanist 521 & Times New Roman

Printed in Hong Kong

contents

introduction

How often have you thought about giving a party and been put off by the idea of preparing and cooking the food involved? Serving drinks is one thing, catering for a crowd is another.

This book has all the answers. Within these pages you will find a complete selection of delectable fingerfoods designed to entertain your guests, no matter what the occasion – formal or informal, outdoors or indoors, no matter what the season.

All recipes are simple to make, use attractive ingredients, easily found on your supermarket shelves and are designed to allow you maximum time to spend with your guests. Most can be prepared beforehand, with little or no last-minute preparation.

The key here is simplicity. Every single recipe in this book is designed to be eaten with fingers only, no forks or knives need be supplied. The only other things that you as the party-giver have to provide are the occasion, good cheer and plenty of napkins.

Some easy hints-using cheese

All foods have a greater appeal if they are attractively presented, and cheese is no exception. Invest in a cheeseboard, or provide a handsome platter and arrange your selection of cheeses in the centre and surround them with a variety of cracker biscuits, celery, radishes or a lovely wreath of fresh fruit. Cheese and fruit are regarded as the perfect after dinner combination by many European gourmets – and for health and sheer good eating we might follow their example.

salmon cucumber bites

cocktail
party

These delicious finger-food recipes

are perfect for your next drinks party. They are easy to make and serve, and taste great!!

salmon
cucumber bites

Photograph page 7

Method:

I   *Place cream cheese, salmon, cream, lemon juice and Tabasco sauce in a food processor and process until smooth. Spoon mixture into a piping bag fitted with a large star nozzle and pipe rosettes onto cucumber slices. Arrange cucumber slices on a serving platter and garnish each with a lemon wedge and a piece of red pepper.*

Makes about 36

ingredients

250g/8oz cream cheese, softened
60g/2oz smoked salmon, chopped
2 tablespoons cream (double)
2 teaspoons lemon juice
1-2 drops Tabasco sauce
2 cucumbers, cut into
5mm/¼in thick slices
I lemon, cut into tiny wedges
¼ red pepper, diced

devils
on horseback

ingredients

30 blanched almonds
30 soft prunes, pitted
**250g/8oz thin rashers bacon,
rind removed**

Method:

I   *Place an almond in the cavity of each prune. Cut bacon into pieces just long enough to wrap around prunes and to overlap slightly. Wrap bacon around prunes and secure with wooden toothpicks or cocktail sticks. Place on a baking tray and bake for 12 minutes or until bacon is crisp. Serve hot.*

Makes 30

Oven temperature 220°C, 425°F, Gas 7

spiced
almonds and pecans

Method:
1 Heat oil in a frying pan over a medium heat, add almonds, pecans and sugar and cook, stirring, until nuts are golden. Transfer to a heatproof bowl.
2 Combine cumin, salt and chilli powder, sprinkle over hot nuts and toss to coat. Cool for 5 minutes, then serve.

Makes 2¹/₂cups/350g/11oz

ingredients

¹/₄ cup/60mL/2fl oz peanut (groundnut) oil
220g/7oz whole blanched almonds
125g/4oz whole pecans
¹/₄ cup/60g/2oz sugar
2 teaspoons ground cumin
1 teaspoon salt
1 teaspoon chilli powder

mini
pizzas

Method:

1 To make dough, place yeast, sugar and water in a bowl and mix to dissolve. Set aside in a warm, draught-free place for 5 minutes or until mixture is foamy.

2 Place flour and salt in a food processor and pulse once or twice to sift. With machine running, slowly pour in yeast mixture and oil and process to make a rough dough. Turn dough onto a lightly floured surface and knead for 5 minutes or until soft and shiny. Add more flour if necessary.

3 Place dough in a lightly oiled bowl and roll around bowl to cover surface with oil. Cover bowl with plastic food wrap and place in a warm, draught-free place for 1-1¹/₂ hours or until doubled in size. Knock down and knead lightly.

4 Divide dough into 4cm/1¹/₂ in balls, press out to make 7cm/2³/₄in circles and place on greased baking trays. Spread each dough circle with tomato paste (passata), then sprinkle with oregano and top with slices of tomato, peperoni or cabanossi and olives. Sprinkle with cheese and bake for 10 minutes or until pizzas are crisp and brown.

Makes about 80

ingredients

Pizza dough
1 teaspoon active dry yeast
pinch sugar
²/₃ cup/170mL/5¹/₂fl oz warm water
2 cups/250g/8oz flour
¹/₂ teaspoon salt
¹/₂ cup/60mL/2fl oz olive oil

Classic pizza topping
³/₄ cup/185g/6oz concentrated tomato paste (passata)
dried oregano leaves
315g/10oz cherry tomatoes, sliced
125g/4oz peperoni or cabanossi, thinly sliced
10-12 pitted black olives, thinly sliced
2 cups/250g/8oz grated mozzarella cheese

Oven temperature 190°C, 375°F, Gas 5

Oven temperature 220°C, 425°F, Gas 7

lobster
filo triangles

Method:

1 To make filling, remove meat from lobster, chop finely and set aside. Melt 45g/1¹/₂oz butter in a saucepan over a medium heat, add spring onions and garlic and cook, stirring, until onions are tender. Stir in flour and cook for 1 minute.

2 Remove pan from heat and whisk in wine and cream, a little at a time, until well blended. Season to taste with cayenne and black pepper, return to heat and cook, stirring constantly, until sauce boils and thickens. Reduce heat to low and simmer for 3 minutes. Remove from heat, stir in lobster meat and cool completely.

3 Cut pastry sheets lengthwise into 5cm/2in wide strips. Working with one strip of pastry at a time, brush pastry with melted butter. Place a teaspoonful of the filling on one end of strip, fold corner of pastry diagonally over filling, then continue folding up the strip to make a neat triangle.

4 Place triangles on a baking tray, brush with butter and bake for 10-15 minutes or until golden.

Makes 24

ingredients

8 sheets filo pastry
125g/4oz butter, melted and cooled

<u>Lobster cream filling</u>
1 cooked lobster
45g/1¹/₂oz butter
6 spring onions, chopped
2 cloves garlic, crushed
1¹/₂ tablespoons flour
¹/₄ cup/60mL/2fl oz white wine
¹/₄ cup/60mL/2fl oz cream (double)
pinch cayenne pepper
freshly ground black pepper

chocolate
macadamia clusters

Method:
1 *Melt chocolate in a bowl over a saucepan of simmering water.*
2 *Chop macadamia nuts into chunks.*
3 *Add nut and shredded coconut to chocolate, stir to coat.*
4 *Place heaped teaspoonfuls mixture onto foil-lined tray, allow to set.*
   Makes about 24

ingredients

300g/10oz dark chocolate, chopped
200g/7oz roasted macadamia nuts
¹/₂ cup/45g/1¹/₂oz shredded coconut

continental
salad sticks

Method:

1 *Slice cucumbers, cut capsicum into squares. Combine vegetables in a bowl.*
2 *Combine dressing ingredients in a screwtop jar, shake well, add to vegetables, stand at least an hour.*
3 *Thread vegetables onto toothpicks or short skewers.*
   Makes 24

ingredients

4 lebanese cucumbers
1 green capsicum (pepper)
250g/8oz punnet cherry tomatoes
24 pitted black olives

Dressing
¹/₃ cup/85ml/3fl oz olive oil
2 tablespoons lemon juice
1 tablespoon chopped fresh basil

oysters
with caviar

Method:

1 Loosen oysters in shell and arrange on large platter. Spoon ¹/₄ teaspoon caviar onto each oyster. Squeeze some lemon juice over each oyster.
2 Cut lemon slices into quarters and present platter with each oyster garnished with a thin piece of lemon. Serve immediately

Makes 24

ingredients

24 oysters on half shell
¹/₄ cup/45g/1¹/₂oz cariar
lemon juice
thin lemon slices

ground
beef filo filling

Method:

1 To make white sauce melt butter in a small saucepan, stir in flour; cook 2 minutes, stirring constantly. Off the heat add milk all at once; return to heat and cook, stirring, until mixture thickens. Simmer 5 minutes. Set aside.
2 Cook onion in butter until golden, add ground beef and cook until meat is brown and juices have evaporated. Add wine, tomatoes, salt and freshly ground black pepper and water. Bring to a boil, reduce heat, cover and simmer until juices have evaporated, about 30 minutes. Cool.
3 Stir ground beef mixture into white sauce. Add cheese and eggs. Use mixture to fill buttered filo sheets.

Makes about 48

ingredients

White sauce
1 tablespoon butter
1¹/₂ tablespoons plain flour
1 cup flour

1 onion, finely chopped
2 tablespoons butter
500g/1lb ground topside beef
³/₄ cup dry white wine
2 tomatoes, peeled, seeded, chopped
1 cup water
salt
pepper
3 hardboiled eggs, chopped
90g/3oz grated Romano cheese

egg
and onion spirals

Method:
1 *To make filling, place eggs in a bowl and mash. Add spring onions, mayonnaise, sour cream and mustard and mix well to combine.*
2 *Make pinwheels as described in recipe for Smoked Ham Pinwheels above.*

Makes 25

ingredients

1 loaf unsliced wholemeal bread
125g/4oz butter, softened

<u>Egg and spring onion filling</u>
8 hard-boiled eggs
4 spring onions, finely chopped
2 tablespoons mayonnaise
2 tablespoons sour cream
2 teaspoons dry mustard

fruit
kebabs

Method:

1 *To make sauce, place mint, honey, sour cream and cream in a bowl and mix to combine. Cover and refrigerate until ready to serve.*
2 *Peel rock melon (cantaloupe), remove seeds and cut into bite-size pieces. Cut kiwifruit in half. Thread two pieces of fruit onto each cocktail stick. Serve with the sauce.*

Makes 16

ingredients

I small rock melon (cantaloupe)
4 kiwifruit, peeled and quartered
250g/8oz strawberries, hulled
16 wooden cocktail sticks

Honey cream sauce
2 tablespoons chopped fresh mint
2 tablespoons honey
I cup/250g/8oz sour cream
I cup/250mL/8fl oz cream (double)

sun-dried
tomato dip

Method:

1 Place sun-dried tomatoes, pine nuts, basil, Parmesan cheese and cream cheese in a food processor or blender and process until smooth. Serve dip with bagel chips or bread and vegetables.

Serving suggestion: Place dip in a bowl on a serving platter or tray and surround with bagel chips or bread and/or raw vegetables.

Serves 4

ingredients

250g/8oz sun-dried tomatoes
60g/2oz pine nuts
3 tablespoons chopped fresh basil
3 tablespoons grated Parmesan cheese
250g/8oz cream cheese, softened
bagel chips or French bread, sliced
selection of raw vegetables such as
cherry tomatoes, celery sticks, carrot
sticks, broccoli florets, cauliflower
florets and green beans

Oven temperature 140°C/280°F/Gas 2

coffee
meringues

ingredients

**³/₄ cup/185g raw sugar
3 tablespoons water
1 egg white
1 teaspoon white vinegar
2 teaspoons cornflour
2 teaspoons coffee essence**

Method:

1 *Place sugar and water in a small saucepan, over a medium heat, stirring until sugar dissolves. Bring to the boil and boil for 1-2 minutes. Brush any sugar grains from sides of pan with a wet pastry brush.*

2 *Beat egg white until stiff peaks form. Continue beating while pouring in hot syrup in a thin stream, a little at a time. Beat until meringue is thick. Fold in vinegar, cornflour and coffee essence.*

3 *Place mixture in a large piping bag fitted with a fluted tube. Pipe 4 cm stars onto greased and lined oven trays. Bake at 140°C/280°F for 1 hour or until firm and dry. Cool in oven with door ajar.*

Note: *Who would believe that these delicious morsels are free of fat and cholesterol? They are perfect to serve with coffee or as an afternoon tea treat.*

Makes 30

spicy
curry dip

Method:

1 Heat oil in a non-stick frypan and cook onion with curry and chilli powders for 4-5 minutes or until onion softens.

2 Whisk into yoghurt and season to taste with pepper. Chill until ready to serve.

Note: *Yoghurt is the ideal base for many dips. When a recipe calls for sour cream replace it with yoghurt to allow those watching their cholesterol to indulge as well. Serve this dip with vegetables such as blanched asparagus spears, raw carrot and celery sticks and cherry tomatoes.*

Makes 1 cup/250mL

ingredients

**2 teaspoons polyunsaturated oil
1 small onion, chopped
1 teaspoon curry powder
pinch chilli powder
1 cup/250mL low fat yoghurt
freshly ground black pepper**

artichoke
hearts stuffed with two cheeses

Method:

1 Slice bottoms off artichoke hearts so they will stand upright.
2 In a small bowl, combine ricotta, Parmesan, capsicum parsley and pepper; mix well.
3 Spoon mixture into the centre of each heart and grill for 1 minute or until the cheese begins to turn golden.

Serves 4

ingredients

500g/1lb jar artichoke hearts, drained
3 tablespoons ricotta cheese
2 tablespoons grated Parmesan cheese
1 tablespoon finely chopped red capsicum (pepper)
1 teaspoon finely chopped parsley
¼ teaspoon black cracked pepper

creamy
oyster dip

Method:

1 *Rinse oysters and place in a small bowl, cover and refrigerate.*

2 *In a small saucepan, over medium heat, combine cream, milk, sour cream, tomato sauce and potato flour. Slowly bring to the boil, stirring constantly until mixture thickens.*

3 *Remove from heat and stir in oysters. Serve with hot toast or biscuits.*

Serves 4

ingredients

24 oysters, removed from shells
1/2 cup cream
1/4 cup milk
1/2 cup sour cream
2 tablespoons tomato sauce
1/4 teaspoon potato flour

cherry
tomatoes with parmesan and rosemary

Photograph page 23

Method:
1 *Sprinkle the inside of tomatoes with black pepper.*
2 *In a small bowl, combine cheese, cream, nutmeg and rosemary, mix well.*
3 *Spoon mixture into the tomatoes and grill for 1 minute. Serve immediately.*
Serves 4

ingredients

**1 punnet cherry tomatoes,
halved and seeded
black pepper
¼ cup grated Parmesan cheese
1 tablespoon cream
pinch nutmeg
1 tablespoon fresh rosemary,
finely chopped**

grilled
eggplant (aubergine) with mozzarella cheese

Photograph page 23

Method:
1 *Lightly brush eggplant slices with combined oil, garlic and pepper. Grill until lightly browned, approximately 3 minutes each side.*
2 *Top each slice with mozzarella cheese and decorate with pimento strips.*
3 *Return to the grill and cook until cheese has melted. Serve immediately and garnish with fresh basil if desired.*
Makes 8

ingredients

**1 medium eggplant (aubergine), cut
into 1cm/½in slices
3 tablespoons olive oil
1 garlic clove, crushed
¼ teaspoon pepper
8 thin slices mozzarella
2 pimentos, sliced into strips**

chilli
onion rings

Method:

1 Blend or process buttermilk and chillies for 30 seconds. Pour mixture into a medium bowl, add onion rings and toss, coating well with buttermilk.

2 Sift flour into a bowl. Using a slotted spoon, transfer onions to the flour. Thoroughly dredge onions in the flour.

3 Heat oil in a deep saucepan and fry onions until golden brown. Keep onions warm in oven at 150°C/300°F/Gas 2. Serve onions with a chilli sauce or chutney.

Serves 4

ingredients

$^1/_2$ **cup buttermilk**
2 chillies, chopped
2 large onions, peeled cut
into $^1/_2$cm/$^1/_4$in rings
2 cups plain flour
2 tablespoons chilli sauce or chutney
oil for deep frying

Oven temperature 150°C/300°F/Gas 2

mussels
au gratin

Method:
1 Combine mussels and 1 cup water in a saucepan, bring to the boil, cook mussels until shells open (about 3 minutes).
2 Remove mussels from water, open shells, discard top shell and loosen mussel meat in shells.
3 In a small bowl combine remaining ingredients, top each mussel with a tablespoon of mixture. Grill for 5 minutes until toppings are golden.

Serves 4

ingredients

24 mussels, cleaned
1 tablespoon fresh basil, chopped
³/₄ cup freshly grated Parmesan cheese
60g/2oz butter, melted
1 cup stale breadcrumbs
2 cloves garlic, crushed

elegant at home party

*tuna with wasabi butter and
baby spinach tarts*

These recipes are ideal for more

These recipes are ideal for more formal entertaining.
Your guests will be impressed when you serve them
such delicacies as Tuna with Wasabi Butter or Smoked
Salmon Mini-Quiches.

27

elegant
at home
party

tuna
with wasabi butter

Photograph page 27

ingredients

250g/8oz tuna steaks, cut 1cm/¹/₂in thick
20 small rounds pumpernickel bread

Ginger marinade
2 teaspoons sesame oil
1 tablespoon soy sauce
1 clove garlic, crushed
2 teaspoons grated fresh ginger

Wasabi butter
75g/2¹/₂oz butter, softened
¹/₂-1 teaspoon wasabi paste or wasabi
powder mixed with water to form a paste
2 tablespoons chopped fresh coriander

Method:
1 *To make marinade, place oil, soy sauce, garlic and ginger in a bowl and mix to combine. Cut tuna into thin slices. Add to marinade and toss to coat. Cover and set aside to marinate for 1 hour. Drain.*
2 *To make Wasabi Butter, place butter, wasabi paste and coriander in a small bowl and beat until smooth.*
3 *Spread pumpernickel rounds with Wasabi Butter, then top with tuna slices. Cover and chill until ready to serve.*
Note: *If fresh tuna is unavailable use fresh salmon fillet*
Makes 20

baby
spinach tarts

Photograph page 27

ingredients

Pastry
1¹/₂ cups/185g/6oz flour
4 tablespoons grated Parmesan cheese
100g/3¹/₂oz butter, chopped
2-3 tablespoons iced water

Spinach filling
2 teaspoons olive oil
2 spring onions, chopped
1 clove garlic, crushed
8 spinach leaves, shredded
125g/4oz ricotta cheese, drained
2 eggs, lightly beaten
¹/₃ cup/90mL/3fl oz milk
¹/₂ teaspoon grated nutmeg
4 tablespoons pine nuts

Method:
1 *To make pastry, place flour, Parmesan cheese and butter in a food processor and process until mixture resembles fine breadcrumbs.*
2 *With machine running, slowly add enough water to form a soft dough. Turn dough onto a lightly floured surface and knead briefly. Wrap dough in plastic food wrap and refrigerate for 30 minutes.*
3 *Roll out pastry to 3mm/¹/₈in thick. Using an 8cm/3¹/₂in fluted pastry cutter, cut out twenty pastry rounds. Place pastry rounds in lightly greased patty tins. Pierce base and sides of pastry with a fork and bake for 5-10 minutes or until lightly golden.*
4 *To make filling, heat oil in a frying pan over a medium heat. Add spring onions, garlic and spinach and cook, stirring, until spinach is wilted. Remove pan from heat and set aside to cool.*
5 *Place spinach mixture, ricotta cheese, eggs, milk and nutmeg in a bowl and mix to combine. Spoon filling into pastry cases and sprinkle with pine nuts. Reduce oven temperature to 180°C/350°F/Gas 4 and bake for 15-20 minutes or until tarts are golden and filling is set.*
Makes 20

crispy
parmesan artichokes

Method:

1 *Remove and discard the tough outer leaves from artichokes (about the first 2 layers). Place artichokes in a saucepan of boiling, lightly salted water, then reduce heat and simmer for 30 minutes or until tender when pierced with a fork.*

2 *Drain artichokes and set aside until cool enough to handle. Remove leaves from artichokes and reserve, leaving hearts intact. Cut hearts into quarters.*

3 *Place Parmesan cheese and breadcrumbs in a shallow dish and mix to combine. Dip bottom halves of leaves and all the hearts into beaten egg, then roll in crumb mixture to coat.*

4 *Heat oil in a saucepan until a cube of bread dropped in browns in 50 seconds and deep-fry leaves and hearts, in batches, for 2 minutes or until golden and crisp. Drain on absorbent kitchen paper.*

Serves 6

ingredients

**3 globe artichokes
125g/4 oz grated Parmesan cheese
1 cup/60g/2oz breadcrumbs, made
from stale bread
4 eggs, lightly beaten
1 cup/250mL/8fl oz olive oil**

Oven temperature 220°C, 425°C, Gas 7

curried
onion puffs

Method:

1 To make puffs, place butter, water and salt in a saucepan over a medium heat and bring to the boil. Remove from heat, add flour all at once and, using a wooden spoon, beat until mixture is smooth.

2 Return pan to heat and cook, stirring constantly, for 3-4 minutes or until mixture leaves the sides of the pan. Remove from heat and beat in eggs, a little at a time, then continue beating until paste is smooth and shiny.

3 Place teaspoons of paste on greased baking trays and bake for 10 minutes. Reduce oven temperature to 180°C/350°F/Gas 4 and bake for 10 minutes or until puffs are crisp and golden.

4 Melt butter in a saucepan over a medium heat, add onions and cook, stirring, for 5 minutes or until onions are golden. Stir in flour and curry powder and cook for 1 minute. Remove pan from heat and slowly stir in cream and black pepper to taste. Return to heat and cook, stirring constantly, until sauce boils and thickens.

5 Make a slit in the side of each puff and spoon filling into cavity. Place filled puffs on a baking tray and bake for 10 minutes or until heated through. Serve immediately.

Makes 24 puffs

ingredients

30g/1oz butter
2 onions, finely chopped
2 teaspoons flour
2 teaspoons curry powder
¹/₂ cup/125mL/4fl oz cream (double)
freshly ground black pepper

<u>Choux puffs</u>
45g/1¹/₂oz butter, cut into pieces
¹/₂ cup/125mL/4fl oz water
pinch salt
¹/₂ cup/60g/2oz flour
2 large eggs, beaten

almond
and cheese grapes

Method:

1 Place cream and blue cheeses and cream in a bowl and beat until smooth. Add grapes to cheese mixture and mix gently to coat.

2 Place almonds in a shallow dish. Using a teaspoon, scoop out grapes, one at a time, place in almonds and roll to coat. Place grapes on a plate, cover and refrigerate until firm.

Makes about 30

ingredients

125g/4oz cream cheese, softened
60g/2oz blue cheese, crumbled
2 tablespoons cream (double)
250g/8oz large seedless green grapes
125g/4oz toasted slivered almonds,
finely chopped

devilled
mixed nuts

Method:

1 *Place nuts and pretzels in a baking dish and mix to combine. Melt butter in a saucepan over a medium heat. Remove pan from heat and stir in garlic, curry and chilli powders and Worcestershire sauce.*

2 *Drizzle butter mixture over nut mixture and mix to coat. Bake at 210°C/420°F, stirring occasionally, for 10 minutes or until mixture is heated through. Serve hot, warm or cold.*

Makes 500g/1 lb

ingredients

375g/12oz mixed nuts
125g/4oz pretzels
60g/2oz butter
2 cloves garlic, crushed
2 teaspoons curry powder
¹/₂ teaspoon chilli powder
2 teaspoons Worcestershire sauce

Oven temperature 210°C/420°F/Gas 6

almond
meringue cream filled cookies

Method:

1 In a medium bowl, and using electric mixer, beat egg whites with sugar until soft peaks form. Fold in ground almonds and cream of tartar.

2 Cover 2 baking trays with greaseproof paper. Drop teaspoons of the mixture, 4cm / 1 1/2in apart on baking trays, smooth the tops and place an almond half on top of biscuit.

3 Bake in moderately slow oven for 20 minutes. Remove from oven and leave to cool on trays for 3 minutes before using a spatula to slide cookies onto a rack to cool.

4 Continue to cook cookies as above, making 25 cookie tops with the almond half on top, and 25 plain cookies for the bases.

5 Whip cream until thick and pipe a circle of cream on top of each base. Top with almond topped cookie.

Makes 25

ingredients

³/₄ **cup sugar**
4 egg whites
³/₄ **cup ground almonds**
¹/₂ **teaspoons cream of tartar**
25 blanched almond halves
I cup cream

Oven temperature 200°C, 400°F, Gas 6

vegetable
samosa

Method:

1 Heat oil in a large frying pan over a medium heat. Add curry powder, onion, mustard seeds and cumin seeds and cook, stirring, for 3 minutes.

2 Add potatoes and stock to pan and cook, stirring occasionally, for 5 minutes or until potatoes are tender.

3 Add carrot and peas to pan and cook for 2 minutes longer. Remove pan from heat and set aside to cool completely.

4 Roll out pastry to 5mm/¹/₄in thick and, using a 10cm/4in pastry cutter, cut out twelve rounds. Place spoonfuls of filling on one half of each pastry round, brush edges with egg, fold uncovered half of pastry over filling and press to seal.

5 Place pastries on lightly greased baking trays, brush with remaining egg and bake for 12-15 minutes or until samosa are puffed and golden.

Makes 12

ingredients

**2 teaspoons vegetable oil
I tablespoon curry powder
I onion, finely chopped
I tablespoon black mustard seeds
2 teaspoons cumin seeds
2 potatoes, finely diced
¹/₂ cup/125mL/4fl oz vegetable stock
I carrot, finely diced
125g/4oz fresh or frozen peas
500g/I lb prepared puff pastry
I egg, lightly beaten**

prawns (shrimp)
with creamy pesto dip

Method:

1 *To make dip, place pesto and mayonnaise in a bowl and mix to combine.*
2 *To serve, place dip in a small bowl on a large serving platter and surround with prawns (shrimp), carrots, snow peas (mangetout) and red pepper.*

Serves 8

ingredients

1 kg/2 lb cooked medium prawns (shrimp), shelled and deveined, tails left intact
2 carrots, cut into thick strips
200g/6¹/₂oz snow peas (mangetout), blanched
1 red pepper, cut into thick strips

Creamy pesto dip
¹/₂ cup/125g/4oz ready-made pesto
¹/₂ cup/125mL/4fl oz whole egg mayonnaise

sweet
chilli parcels

ingredients

200g/6¹/₂oz pork mince
4 spring onions, chopped
1 carrot, grated
2 tablespoons soy sauce
3 tablespoons crunchy peanut butter
24 spring roll or wonton wrappers,
each 12¹/₂cm/5in square
vegetable oil for deep-frying
sweet chilli sauce

Method:

1 *Heat a nonstick frying pan over a high heat, add pork and cook, stirring, for 5 minutes or until browned.*

2 *Add spring onions, carrot, soy sauce and peanut butter to pan and cook, stirring, for 2 minutes longer. Remove pan from heat and set aside to cool completely.*

3 *Place spoonfuls of mixture in the centre of each spring roll or wonton wrapper, then draw the corners together and twist to form small bundles.*

4 *Heat oil in a large saucepan until a cube of bread dropped in browns in 50 seconds. Cook bundles a few at a time for 3-4 minutes or until golden. Drain and serve with sweet chilli sauce.*

Makes 16

pickled
quail eggs

ingredients

8 cups/2 litres/70fl oz white vinegar
2 dried red chillies
12 whole cardamom pods
¹/₃ cup/45g/1¹/₂oz coriander seeds
10 cloves
1 teaspoon tumeric
8 cloves garlic
1 teaspoon salt
1 large onion
36 quail eggs

Method:

1 *Combine vinegar and chillies in a large saucepan, add cardamom, coriander, cloves, turmeric, garlic and salt, bring mixture to a boil, reduce heat, cover and simmer 5 minutes. Take off the heat and cool. Strain*

2 *Slice onion thinly. Hard boil eggs, about 3 minutes, and plunge into cold water straight away. Shell and place in 1.5 litre/6 cup parfait jar with onion. Pour vinegar over, make sure eggs are completely covered. Cover jar and keep in dark place 1 week before using.*

Makes 36

curry
puffs with minted yoghurt

Method:

1 Place cumin and coriander in a nonstick frying pan and cook over a high heat, stirring, for 1 minute. Add curry paste and onions and cook, stirring for 2 minutes longer.

2 Add lamb or beef and cook, stirring, for 4 minutes or until browned. Remove pan from heat and set aside to cool.

3 Roll out pastry to 3mm/^{1}/$_8$in thick and, using a 5cm/2in round pastry cutter, cut out sixteen circles. Place a spoonful of meat mixture on one half of each pastry circle. Fold pastry over to encase meat mixture, then press edges together with a fork to seal.

4 Place pastries on a lightly greased baking tray and bake for 10-12 minutes or until golden brown.

5 To make Minted yoghurt, place yoghurt, mint and cumin in a small bowl and mix to combine. Serve with warm Curry Puffs.

Makes 16

ingredients

1 teaspoon ground cumin
1 teaspoon ground coriander
2 teaspoons mild curry paste
2 onions, chopped
250g/8oz ground lamb or beef
500g/1 lb prepared puff pastry

<u>Minted yoghurt</u>
1 cup/200g/6^1/$_2$oz natural yoghurt
4 tablespoons chopped fresh mint
1 teaspoon ground cumin

Oven temperature 180°C, 350°F, Gas 4

37

elegant
at home
party

elegant at home party
elegant at home party

Oven temperature 220°C, 425°F, Gas 7

featherlight
scones

Method:

1 Place flour, sugar and salt in a bowl and mix to combine. Using fingertips, rub in butter until mixture resembles fine breadcrumbs. Add milk and water all at once and, using a rounded knife, mix lightly and quickly to make a soft, sticky dough.

2 Turn dough onto a lightly floured surface and knead lightly until smooth. Press out to make 3cm/1¼in thick rectangle and using 5cm/2in scone cutter, cut out rounds.

3 Place scones, just touching, in a greased shallow 18x28cm/7x11in baking tin. Brush with milk and bake for 12-15 minutes or until scones are well risen and golden. Transfer to wire racks to cool.

4 To serve, split scones and top with jam or lemon butter (curd) and cream, if desired.

Makes about 20

ingredients

4 cups/500 g/1 lb self-raising flour, sifted
2 tablespoons caster sugar
¼ teaspoon salt
60g/2oz butter
1 cup/250mL/8fl oz buttermilk
¾ cup/185mL/6fl oz water
milk for glazing
jam or lemon butter (curd)
whipped cream (optional)

smoked
salmon mini quiches

Method:
1 Roll out pastry to 3mm/^{1}/₈in thick and using a 6cm/2^1/₂in pastry cutter, cut out twenty-four rounds. Press pastry rounds into shallow, greased patty pans (tartlet tins).
2 To make filling, place eggs, cream, nutmeg and black pepper to taste in a bowl and whisk to combine. Stir in salmon and dill.
3 Divide filling between pastry cases and bake for 10-15 minutes or until quiches are puffed and golden.
Makes 24

ingredients

185g/6oz prepared puff pastry

Salmon cream filling
6 eggs, lightly beaten
1^1/₂ cups/375mL/12fl oz cream (double)
^{1}/₄ teaspoon ground nutmeg
freshly ground black pepper
125g/4oz smoked salmon, chopped
2 teaspoons chopped fresh dill

Oven temperature 190°C, 375°F, Gas 5

chocolate
pecan brownies

Method:

1 Place corn or golden syrup and sugar in a saucepan over a medium heat and cook, stirring, until sugar dissolves and mixture boils. Remove pan from heat, stir in chocolate and butter and continue stirring until mixture is smooth. Beat in eggs and rum.

2 Place pecans and flour in a bowl and mix to combine. Add chocolate mixture and mix to combine.

3 Spread mixture into a greased and lined 18x28cm/7x11in shallow cake tin and bake for 25-30 minutes or until brownies are set.

4 Stand brownies in tin for 10 minutes, then turn onto a wire rack to cool. To serve, dust brownies with icing sugar, cut into small squares and top each with a strawberry half.

Makes 24

ingredients

¹/₂ cup/125mL/4fl oz dark corn or golden syrup
¹/₄ cup/60g/2oz sugar
90g/3oz dark chocolate, chopped
45g/1¹/₂oz butter
2 eggs, lightly beaten
1 tablespoon dark rum
185g/6oz pecan nuts, finely chopped
¹/₂ cup/60g/2oz flour
1 tablespoon icing sugar
12 strawberries, halved

Oven temperature 180°C, 350°F, Gas 4

Oven temperature 220°C/425°F/Gas 7

cheese
and chive cookies

Method:

1 Place flour, butter, blue and Parmesan cheeses and chives in a food processor and process until ingredients cling together. Turn onto a lightly floured surface and knead lightly. Shape dough into a ball, wrap in plastic food wrap and chill for 30 minutes.

2 Roll heaped teaspoons of mixture into balls, then roll in sesame seeds to coat. Place balls on lightly greased baking trays, flatten slightly with a fork and bake for 10 minutes at 220°C/425°F or until golden. Stand on trays for 3 minutes, then tranfer to wire racks to cool. Store cookies in an airtight container.

Makes 30

ingredients

1 cup/125g/4oz self-raising flour, sifted
125g/4oz butter, cut into pieces
60g/2oz hard blue cheese, crumbled
2 tablespoons grated Parmesan cheese
3 tablespoons snipped fresh chives
4 tablespoons sesame seeds

summer
lunch
party

bacon wrapped prawns

summer lunch party

In the midst of a hot summer day,

these wonderful nibbles will be enjoyed by one and all.

pistachio
cheese balls

Method:
1 Combine butter, cream cheese, curry powder, tabasco, soy, mustard and Worcestershire in food processor. Blend until smooth. Add salt and freshly ground black pepper to taste. Spoon into a bowl, cover and refrigerate until stiff.
2 Shape into balls the size of a walnut, roll in chopped pistachios. Refrigerate until ready to serve.
Makes about 60

ingredients

¹/₂ cup/120g/4oz butter
250g/8oz cream cheese
1 teaspoon mild curry powder
1 teaspoon tabasco sauce
1 teaspoon light soy sauce
1 teaspoon mustard powder
1 tablespoon Worcestershire sauce
1 cup/10g/4oz finely chopped pistachio
nuts
salt
pepper

bacon
wrapped prawns (shrimp)

Photograph page 43

Method:
1 To make marinade, place oregano, garlic, oil and vinegar in a bowl and whisk to combine. Add prawns and toss to coat. Cover and refrigerate for at least 1 hour or overnight.
2 Drain prawns (shrimp) and reserve marinade. Cut each bacon rasher into three pieces, wrap a piece of bacon around each prawn (shrimp) and secure with a wooden toothpick or cocktail stick.
3 Cook prawns (shrimp) under a preheated medium grill or on the barbecue, turning occasionally and brushing with reserved marinade for 5 minutes or until bacon is crisp and prawns (shrimp) are cooked.
Makes about 24

ingredients

750g/1¹/₂1b large uncooked prawns (shrimp), shelled and deveined, tails left intact
8 rashers bacon, rind removed

Herb marinade
2 tablespoons chopped fresh oregano
2 cloves garlic, crushed
¹/₂ cup/125mL/4fl oz olive oil
2 tablespoons white wine vinegar

marinated
mushrooms

Method:

1 Trim stalks from mushrooms and wipe with a clean damp teatowel. Place mushrooms in a bowl, pour over boiling water and lemon juice and stand for 5 minutes.

2 To make marinade, place parsley, thyme, garlic, oil, vinegar and black pepper to taste in a screwtop jar and shake to combine.

3 Drain mushrooms, return to bowl, pour over marinade, cover and marinate in the refrigerator for at least 2 hours or overnight.

Makes about 30

ingredients

500g/1 lb button mushrooms
1 cup/250mL/8fl oz boiling water
2 tablespoons lemon juice

<u>Mushroom marinade</u>
1 tablespoon chopped fresh parsley
2 teaspoons chopped fresh thyme
2 cloves garlic, crushed
¹/₃ cup/90mL/3fl oz olive oil
2 tablespoons white wine vinegar
freshly ground black pepper

Oven temperature 150°C/300°F/Gas 2

coconut
lemon wedges

Method:

1 Combine macaroons, coconut and Cointreau, press evenly over base of a 23cm/9in springform pan.

2 Cream butter, lemon rind and sugar in small bowl with electric mixer until light and fluffy. Beat in eggs, one at a time (mixture may curdle but is not a problem). Stir in lemon juice and coconut. Spread over macaroon base.

3 Bake in slow oven (150°C/300°F/Gas 2, for about 40 minutes or until golden brown, cool. Remove sides of pan, cut into wedges to serve.

Makes about 15 wedges

ingredients

¹/₃ cup crushed coconut macaroons
³/₄ cup coconut
¹/₄ cup Cointreau Liqueur
90g/3oz butter
2 teaspoons grated lemon rind
¹/₂ cup castor sugar
2 eggs
2 tablespoons lemon juice
1¹/₄ cups coconut

snow peas
with herb cheese filling

Method:

1 Cook snow peas (mangetout) in boiling water for 20 seconds, drain, and rinse under cold water. Split snow peas along the curved side, leaving the straight side intact.

2 Blend or process combined cream cheese, parsley, dill, garlic and pepper until smooth. Spoon into a piping bag fitted with a small star pipe.

3 Pipe herb mixture into snow peas, refrigerate until firm. Garnish with chilli.

Makes 24

ingredients

24 snow peas (mangetout)
125g/4oz cream cheese, softened
2 tablespoons chopped parsley
1 tablespoon chopped dill
2 cloves garlic, crushed
freshly ground black pepper
2 red chillies, finely chopped

guacamole

Method:

1 Cut avocados in half, remove seeds and skin. Mash avocados roughly with a fork.
2. Plunge tomatoes into boiling water for 30 seconds, remove. Peel off skin, cut into quarters, remove and discard seeds. Cut tomatoes into small dice.
3 Combine avocado, tomato, onion, chilli, coriander and lemon juice. Serve with corn chips for dipping.

Serves 8

ingredients

3 avocados
2 small tomatoes
1 small onion, very finely chopped
3 red chillies, chopped
2 tablespoons chopped fresh coriander
2 tablespoons lemon juice
2 x 200g/6¹/₂oz pkts corn chips

crunchy
split pea snacks

Method:
1 Wash peas under cold running water, drain. Place peas in a bowl, cover with cold water, stir in soda, stand overnight.
2 Drain peas, wash thoroughly under cold, running water, drain well. Drain again on absorbent paper.
3 Deep fry in 4 batches in heated oil, until golden brown, drain on absorbent paper.
4 Combine peas in a bowl with curry, cumin, chilli, and allow to cool.

Makes about 3 cups

ingredients

¹/₂ cup green split peas
¹/₂ cup yellow split peas
2 teaspoons bicarbonate of soda
oil for deep frying
1 teaspoon curry powder
1 teaspoon ground cumin
¹/₂ teaspoon chilli powder

hazelnut
bread

Method:

1 Beat egg whites in a small bowl with electric mixer until soft peaks form. Gradually add sugar 1 tablespoon at a time, beat until dissolved between additions.

2 Fold in flour and hazelnuts, spread evenly into a greased and lined bar pan 7cmx25cm/ 2³/₄inx10in.

3 Bake in moderate oven 180°C/350°/Gas 4 for 30 minutes or until light golden brown. Turn onto wire rack to cool. Wrap in foil, stand overnight.

4 Using an electric knife or very sharp knife, slice loaf thinly. Bake slices on an oven tray in a slow oven for 45 minutes or until dry and crisp. Store in airtight container for up to 1 month.

Makes about 48 slices

ingredients

3 egg whites
¹/₂ cup castor sugar
1 cup plain flour
150g/5oz roasted hazelnuts

Oven temperature 180°C/350°F/Gas 4

carpaccio

Method:

1 Ask your butcher to cut the fillet into paper thin slices
2 Cut breadstick into 1cm/¹/₂in slices, place in single layer on a baking tray, bake in moderate slow oven 150°C/325°F/Gas 3 for 10 minutes or until bread is crisp but not dry, cool.
3 Spread thinly with combined butter, cheese and rind.
4 Place a slice of beef fillet onto each bread slice, top with a little tartare sauce, anchovy and capers, garnish with parsley.

Makes about 60

ingredients

500g/1lb piece beef eye fillet
2 breadsticks
90g/3oz butter
2 tablespoons grated Parmesan cheese
2 teaspoons grated lemon rind
¹/₃ cup tartare sauce
1 tablespoon chopped anchovy fillets
2 tablespoons chopped capers
parsley to garnish

artichoke
bread savouries

Method:
1 *Drain artichokes, cut in half.*
2 *Cut bread slices into circles using a 4cm/
1¹/₂in cutter. Deep-fry circles in heated oil
until golden brown, drain.*
3 *Combine mayonnaise, cream and chives.*
4 *To assemble place 1 or 2 artichoke halves
(depending on their size) onto bread circles.
Drizzle with a little mayonnaise mixture,
garnish with chopped pimento and dill.*
Makes 12

ingredients

**240g/8oz can artichoke hearts
12 slices bread
oil for deep-frying
¹/₄ cup mayonnaise
1 tablespoon thickened cream
1 tablespoon chopped chives
2 tablespoons chopped pimento
dill for garnish**

taramosalata

Method:

1 Peel and chop potatoes, cook in boiling water until tender, drain, cool.
2 Remove crusts from bread, combine in a bowl with 1 cup water, stand 2 minutes, strain, press out excess water.
3 Place potatoes, bread, tarama, onion and pepper in a blender or processor, blend until smooth.
4 With blender running, gradually pour in combined olive oil and lemon juice, blend until combined.
5 Split pita bread in half, cut each half into wedges, serve with taramosalata.

Serves 8

ingredients

250g/¹/₂lb potatoes
6 slices white bread
100g/3¹/₂oz can tarama or 60g/2oz fresh
1 onion, finely grated
freshly ground black pepper
¹/₂ cup olive oil
¹/₂ cup lemon juice
4 slices pita bread

Oven temperature 220°C/440°F/Gas 7

sesame
twists

Method:

1 *Cut pastry sheets in half, brush with melted butter.*
2 *Combine poppy seeds, sesame seeds and cheese, sprinkle over pastry, press firmly into pastry with a rolling pin.*
3 *Using a sharp knife, cut widthwise into strips, 2cm/³/4in wide and 10cm/4in long. Twist strips slightly.*
4 *Place onto lightly greased baking trays; bake in hot oven 220°C/440°F/Gas 7, for 8 minutes or until puffed and golden brown.*

Makes 48 twists

ingredients

2 sheets ready-rolled puff pastry
60g/2oz butter, melted
2 tablespoons poppy seeds
2 tablespoons sesame seeds
2 tablespoons grated Parmesan cheese

oyster
cases with leek chiffonade

Method:

1 *Slice white part of leeks, discard green. Melt butter in a frying pan; add leeks and fennel, stirfry over low heat until tender, about 10 minutes.*
2 *Add cream, sour cream, salt and pepper, simmer 5 minutes or until reduced and thickened slightly.*
3 *Spoon mixture into oyster cases, sprinkle with Parmesan cheese, bake in moderate oven 180°C/350°F/Gas 4 for 10 minutes or until heated through.*

Makes 16

ingredients

2 leeks
¹/₂ fennel bulb, chopped
30g/1oz butter
¹/₃ cup cream
¹/₃ cup sour cream
salt
pepper
16 puff pastry oyster cases
2 tablespoons grated Parmesan cheese

Oven temperature 180°C/350°F/Gas 4

55

deep-fried
crab balls

Method:

1 To make sauce, place onion, parsley, basil, gherkins, olives, mustard, mayonnaise and black pepper to taste in a bowl and mix to combine. Cover and refrigerate until required.

2 Place crabmeat, breadcrumbs, butter, mustard, egg yolks, Tabasco sauce and black pepper to taste in a bowl and mix to combine. Cover and chill until mixture is firm.

3 Shape mixture into walnut-sized balls, place on a plate lined with nonstick baking paper, cover and chill for 30 minutes.

4 Heat oil in a large saucepan until a cube of bread dropped in browns in 50 seconds. Roll crab balls in flour to coat, shake off excess and deep-fry in hot oil, in batches, for 2-3 minutes or until golden. Drain on absorbent kitchen paper and serve warm with Tartare Sauce (see below).

Makes about 36

ingredients

500g/1 lb crabmeat, flaked
½ cup/30g/1oz breadcrumbs,
made from stale bread
60g/2oz butter, softened
1 tablespoon Dijon mustard
2 egg yolks
few drops Tabasco sauce
freshly ground black pepper
vegetable oil for deep-frying
flour for coating

tartare
sauce

Method:

1 Combine all ingredients.

ingredients

Sauce tartare
1 teaspoon finely chopped onion
1 teaspoon chopped fresh parsley
1 teaspoon chopped fresh basil
1 teaspoon finely chopped gherkins
1 teaspoon finely chopped green olives
1 teaspoon Dijon mustard
1 cup/250mL/8fl oz good quality egg
mayonnaise

smoked
salmon bagels

Method:

1 Spread each bagel half with cream cheese and sprinkle with chives. Top bagel halves with salmon, onion, avocado and capers. Sprinkle with lemon juice and serve immediately.

Serving suggestion: *A tomato and onion salad is a delicious side dish. To make salad, arrange sliced tomatoes and very thinly sliced onion on a lettuce lined dish. Sprinkle with chopped fresh basil and drizzle with French dressing. Season to taste with black pepper.*

Serves 4

ingredients

4 bagels, split
125g/4oz cream cheese, softened
2 tablespoons snipped fresh chives
250g/8oz smoked salmon slices
1 onion, thinly sliced
1 avocado, stoned, peeled and sliced
1 tablespoon capers, drained
1 tablespoon lemon juice

double
dipped chocolate strawberries

Method:
1 Melt white chocolate with half the copha in a bowl over saucepan of simmering water.
2 Hold strawberries by the stem; dip $^2/_3$ of the strawberry into chocolate. Hold over chocolate to allow excess to run off. Place onto a foil covered tray, refrigerate until set.
3 Melt dark chocolate with remaining copha in a bowl over a saucepan of simmering water.
4 Dip strawberries into chocolate, $^2/_3$ of the way up the white chocolate. Hold over chocolate to allow excess to run off. Place onto foil covered tray, refrigerate until set.

Makes about 52

ingredients

125g/4oz white chocolate
60g/2oz copha (vegetable shortening)
2 x 250g/¹/₂lb punnets strawberries
125g/4oz dark chocolate

prawn
(shrimp) toast

Method:

1 Peel and devein prawns, combine in a blender or processor with spring onions, ginger, soy sauce and sesame oil, blend until roughly chopped. Add egg whites, blend until combined.
2 Remove crusts from bread slices, spread with prawn mixture.
3 Cut each slice into 3 strips. Dip prawn coated side of each strip into breadcrumbs.
4 Deep-fry in heated oil until light golden brown, drain on absorbent paper, serve immediately.

Makes 18

ingredients

500g/1lb cooked prawns (shrimps)
6 spring onions (scallions), chopped
2 teaspoons grated fresh ginger
2 teaspoons light soy sauce
¹/₂ teaspoon sesame oil
2 egg whites
6 slices white bread
¹/₂ cup fresh breadcrumbs
oil for deep-frying

*thai barbecue fish cakes and
antipasto skewers*

barbecue
party

What better way to entertain than

*with an informal barbecue? On a beautiful and
relaxing day, these tasty recipes will have your guests
coming back for more.*

thai
barbecue fish cakes
Photograph page 61

Method:
1 Place fish, curry paste, lemon grass, coriander, lime leaves and egg white in a food processor and process until smooth.
2 Using wet or lightly oiled hands, take 1 tablespoon of mixture and roll into a ball, then flatten to form a disk. Repeat with remaining mixture. Place fish cakes on a tray lined with plastic food wrap and chill for 30 minutes or until firm.
3 Preheat barbecue to a high heat. Place fish cakes on oiled barbecue plate (griddle) and cook for 1 minute each side or until cooked through. Serve with lime wedges and sweet chilli sauce.

Makes 18

ingredients

375g/12oz boneless, fine fleshed, white fish fillets, chopped
2 tablespoons red curry paste
1 stalk fresh lemon grass, chopped or
½ teaspoon dried lemon grass, soaked in hot water until soft
1 tablespoon chopped fresh coriander
4 kaffir lime leaves, finely shredded
1 egg white
lime wedges
sweet chilli sauce

antipasto
skewers
Photograph page 61

Method:
1 Place rosemary leaves, thyme leaves, vinegar and oil in a bowl and whisk to combine. Cut eggplant (aubergines) and zucchini (courgettes) into cubes. Add to vinegar mixture, then add tomatoes and red pepper (capsicum). Toss to coat vegetables with marinade, cover and marinate for 30-60 minutes.
2 To make dipping sauce, place pesto, sour cream and black pepper to taste in a bowl and mix to combine.
3 Preheat barbecue to a high heat. Roll salami slices tightly. Drain vegetables and reserve marinade. Thread vegetables and salami rolls, alternately, onto small skewers. Cook skewers, brushing frequently with reserved marinade, on oiled barbecue grill for 1-2 minutes each side or until vegetables are tender. Serve skewers warm with dipping sauce.

Makes 12

ingredients

1 tablespoon fresh rosemary leaves
1 tablespoon fresh thyme leaves
¼ cup/60mL/2fl oz balsamic vinegar
2 tablespoons olive oil
2 baby eggplant (aubergines), halved lengthwise
2 zucchini (courgettes), halved lengthwise
155g/5oz semi-dried tomatoes
1 red pepper (capsicum), diced
250 g/8 oz sliced spicy salami

Creamy pesto dipping sauce
¼ cup/60mL/2fl oz pesto
½ cup/125g/4oz sour cream
freshly ground black pepper

marinated
seared tuna

Method:
1 Preheat barbecue to a high heat.
2 Brush tuna with sesame oil. Place tuna on oiled barbecue grill and cook for 5 seconds each side - the outside of the tuna should be seared only and the centre still uncooked.
3 To make marinade, place spring onions, parsley, ginger, soy sauce, lemon juice in a shallow dish. Place tuna in marinade, turn to coat, cover and marinate in the refrigerator, turning occasionally, for 1-2 hours.
4 To serve, remove tuna from marinade and cut into thin slices. Arrange tuna slices attractively on a serving platter and spoon over a little of the marinade.

Serves 12

ingredients

375g/12oz piece sashimi tuna
2 teaspoons sesame oil

<u>Ginger and lemon marinade</u>
2 spring onions, minced
1 tablespoon finely chopped
flat-leaf parsley
2 teaspoons minced fresh ginger
¹/₄ cup/60mL/2fl oz soy sauce
2 tablespoons lemon juice

grilled
strawberry kebabs

Method:
1 *Preheat barbecue to a high heat.*
2 *Thread strawberries onto lighlty oiled wooden skewers. Brush strawberries with vinegar, then roll in icing sugar. Cook kebabs on oiled barbecue grill for 10 seconds each side or until icing sugar caramelises. Serve immediately with ice cream.*

Note: *Remember to soak bamboo or wooden skewers in water before using - this helps to prevent them from burning during cooking. Before threading food onto skewers, lightly oil them so that the cooked food is easy to remove. For this recipe, use a light tasting oil such as canola or sunflower.*

Serves 8

ingredients

500g/1 lb strawberries, halved
¼ cup/60 mL/2 fl oz balsamic vinegar
1½ cups/220g/7oz icing sugar
vanilla ice cream

tomato
salsa on bruschetta

Method:

1 Preheat barbecue to a medium heat. To make the dressing, place garlic cloves on barbecue plate (griddle) and cook for 1-2 minutes each side or until flesh is soft. Squeeze flesh from garlic cloves and mash. Place garlic, vinegar and oil in a screwtop jar and shake to combine.

2 To make salsa, place tomatoes and 2 tablespoons oil in a bowl and toss to coat. Place tomatoes, cut side down, on barbecue plate (griddle) and cook for 1 minute each side. Place tomatoes, cheese, basil and black peppercorns to taste in a bowl, add dressing and toss to combine.

3 Lightly brush bread with oil, place on barbecue grill and toast for 1 minute each side. To serve, pile tomato salsa onto bread and serve immediately.

Makes 12

ingredients

12 slices crusty Italian bread

Grilled tomato salsa
500g/1 lb cherry tomatoes, halved olive oil
6 small bocconcini cheeses, chopped
4 tablespoons torn fresh basil leaves
crushed black peppercorns

Roasted garlic dressing
2 garlic cloves, unpeeled
2 tablespoons balsamic vinegar
1 tablespoon olive oil

lamb
and mango skewers

Method:

1 *To make marinade, place ginger, hoisin and soy sauces, vinegar and oil in a bowl and mix to combine. Add lamb, toss to coat, cover and marinate in the refrigerator for at least 4 hours.*

2 *Thread lamb and mango cubes, alternately, onto oiled skewers. Cook on a preheated hot barbecue for 3-4 minutes each side or until tender.*

Serves 8

ingredients

1 kg/2 lb lean lamb, trimmed of visible fat and cut into 2cm/³/₄in cubes
3 mangoes, cut into 2cm/³/₄in cubes

<u>Hoisin Soy Marinade</u>
1 tablespoon finely grated fresh ginger
³/₄ cup/185mL/6fl oz hoisin sauce
¹/₄ cup/60mL/2fl oz reduced-salt soy sauce
¹/₄ cup/60mL/2fl oz rice wine vinegar
¹/₄ cup/60mL/2fl oz vegetable oil

spicy
chicken satays

Method:

1 Place onions, lemon rind, ginger, garlic, coriander, cumin and oil in a food processor and process to make a paste. Transfer mixture to a bowl, add chicken and toss to coat. Cover and marinate at room temperature for 1 hour or in the refrigerator overnight.

2 To make sauce, place onion, chillies and peanuts in a food processor or blender and process to make a paste. Heat oil in a saucepan over a medium heat, add onion mixture and cook, stirring, for 5 minutes. Add tamarind sauce and water and bring to the boil. Reduce heat to low and simmer until sauce reduces and thickens.

3 Drain chicken and thread onto oiled skewers. Cook kebabs on a preheated hot barbecue for 5-6 minutes each side or until chicken is tender. Serve with Peanut Sauce.

Serves 8

ingredients

2 onions, chopped
1 tablespoon grated lemon rind
2 teaspoons finely grated fresh ginger
2 cloves garlic, crushed
1 teaspoon ground coriander
1 teaspoon ground cumin
$^1/_4$ cup/60mL/2fl oz vegetable oil
6 boneless chicken breast fillets,
cut into 2cm/$^3/_4$in cubes

Peanut Sauce
1 onion, chopped
6 fresh red chillies, chopped
155g/5oz peanuts
$^1/_4$ cup/60mL/2fl oz vegetable oil
1 tablespoon tamarind sauce
$^3/_4$ cup/185mL/6fl oz water

marinated
beef strips

Method:

1 *To make marinade, place onion, garlic, parsley, thyme, black peppercorns, wine and oil in a bowl and mix to combine. Add beef, toss to coat, cover and marinate in the refrigerator for at least 4 hours.*

2 *Drain beef and reserve marinade. Weave beef strips onto oiled skewers, then cook on a preheated hot barbecue grill, brushing frequently with marinade and turning, for 2-3 minutes or until cooked to your liking.*

Serves 8

ingredients

I kg/2 lb beef rump steak, trimmed of visible fat and cut into long strips

<u>**Garlic Wine Marinade**</u>
I large onion, sliced
4 cloves garlic, chopped
4 tablespoons chopped fresh parsley
I tablespoon fresh thyme leaves
I tablespoon black peppercorns
I cup/250mL/8fl oz dry red wine
¹/₃ cup/90mL/3fl oz olive oil

tangy
veal skewers

Method:

1 To make marinade, place oil, lemon juice, vinegar, capers and tarragon in a bowl and mix to combine. Add veal, toss to coat, cover and marinate in the refrigerator for at least 4 hours.

2 Cook onions in a saucepan of boiling water for 5 minutes. Drain, cool and cut in half. Drain veal and reserve marinade. Thread veal and onions, alternately, onto oiled skewers.

3 Brush kebabs with reserved marinade and cook on preheated hot barbecue for 2-3 minutes each side or until veal is tender.

Serves 8

ingredients

1 kg/2 lb veal steak, trimmed of visible fat and cut into thin strips
8-12 small pickling onions

Tangy Marinade
$^1/_2$ cup/125mL/4fl oz olive oil
$^1/_4$ cup/60mL/2fl oz lemon juice
2 tablespoons white wine vinegar
3 tablespoons drained capers
2 tablespoons chopped fresh tarragon

basil
and prawn (shrimp) skewers

Method:

1 *To make marinade, place basil, peppercorns, oil, wine and lemon juice in a screwtop jar and shake to combine. Place prawns (shrimp) in a non-reactive bowl, pour over marinade and toss to coat. Cover and marinate in the refrigerator for 2-6 hours.*

2 *Drain prawns (shrimp) and reserve marinade. Thread prawns (shrimp) and lemon slices, alternately, onto oiled skewers. Cook kebabs on a preheated hot barbecue grill, basting with marinade, for 3 minutes each side or until prawns (shrimp) change colour. Scatter with chopped basil and serve.*

Serves 8

ingredients

1 ½-1 ¾ kg/3-3 ¼ lb medium uncooked prawns (shrimp), shelled and deveined, tails left intact
24 slices lemon
3-4 tablespoons chopped fresh basil

Basil Marinade
4-6 tablespoons chopped fresh basil
1 tablespoon crushed black peppercorns
1 cup/250mL/8fl oz olive oil
¾ cup/185mL/6fl oz dry white wine
¼ cup/60mL/2fl oz lemon juice

raspberry
marinated chicken wings

Method:

1 *Combine oil, vinegar, honey, sesame seeds, cumin, salt and garlic in a screwtop jar, shake until well combined. Pour over chicken wings, cover, refrigerate overnight.*

2 *Remove from marinade and barbecue until cooked through and crisp, brushing with the marinade and turning from time to time.*

Makes 24

ingredients

24 chicken wings

Raspberry marinade
1 cup/250ml/8fl oz olive oil
⅓ cup/85ml/3fl oz raspberry vinegar
1 tablespoon honey
1 tablespoon sesame seeds
1 teaspoon cumin
½ teaspoon salt
2 cloves garlic, crushed

prosciutto
melon

Method:

I *Cut rock melon (cantaloupe) in half lengthwise and scoop out seeds. Cut each half into 8 wedges, remove skin and cut in half, crosswise. Cut each slice of prosciutto or ham, lengthwise into 3 strips and wrap one strip around each piece of melon. Arrange on a serving plate, cover and chill.*

Makes 32

ingredients

**I rock melon (cantaloupe)
250g/8oz very thinly sliced
prosciutto or lean ham**

herb-filled
cherry tomatoes

Method:

1 Cut tops off tomatoes and carefully scoop out seeds. Reserve 2 tablespoons of the pulp. Place tomatoes up side down on absorbent kitchen paper and drain.

2 To make filling, place cream cheese in a food processor and process until light and fluffy. Add reserved tomato pulp, mint, parsley, chives, almonds and black pepper to taste and process briefly to combine.

3 Spoon or pipe filling into tomato shells and arrange on a serving platter. Cover and refrigerate for 1 hour or until firm.

Makes about 36

ingredients

500g/1 lb cherry tomatoes

Herb Cheese Filling
125g/4oz cream cheese, softened
1 tablespoon chopped fresh mint
1 tablespoon chopped fresh parsley
1 tablespoon snipped fresh chives
45g/1¹/₂oz slivered almonds, toasted
freshly ground black pepper

Method:

1 To make pastry, place flour and icing sugar in a food processor and process to combine. Add butter and process until mixture resembles fine breadcrumbs. With machine running, add egg yolks and water and process to form a rough dough. Turn dough out onto a lightly floured surface and knead until smooth. Wrap dough in plastic food wrap and chill for 20 minutes.

2 Roll out dough to 3mm/¹/₈in thick. Using an 8cm/3¹/₄in pastry cutter, cut out eighteen rounds. Place pastry rounds in lightly greased patty pans (tartlet tins). Prick base and sides of pastry with a fork and bake for 10 minutes or until golden. Cool on a wire rack.

3 To make custard filling, place sugar, cornflour, eggs and egg yolk in a bowl and whisk until smooth and thick. Heat milk and cream in a saucepan over a medium heat, then gradually whisk in egg mixture. Reduce heat to low and cook, stirring constantly, until mixtures boils and thickens. Remove pan from heat, stir in liqueur, cover and set aside to cool.

4 To assemble, place gelatine and boiling water in a bowl and stir until gelatine dissolves. Stir in sieved jam and liqueur and set aside until glaze cools and begins to thicken. Spoon filling into pastry shells, then decorate with fruit and brush tops with gelatine mixture. Chill until firm.

Makes 18

Oven temperature 190°C, 375°F, Gas 5

fruit
tartlets

ingredients

1 teaspoon gelatine
¹/₃ cup/90mL/3fl oz boiling water
¹/₂ cup/155g/5oz apricot jam, warmed and sieved
2 teaspoons orange-flavoured liqueur
440g/14oz canned apricot halves, drained and sliced
12 strawberries, halved or sliced
125g/4oz seedless green or black grapes, halved
2 peaches, sliced
2 kiwifruit, sliced

Rich pastry
1¹/₂ cups/185g/6oz flour
2 tablespoons icing sugar
125g/4oz butter
2 egg yolks
1 teaspoon water

Custard cream filling
¹/₂ cup/125g/4oz sugar
6 teaspoons cornflour
2 eggs
1 egg yolk
³/₄ cup/185mL/6fl oz milk
¹/₄ cup/6 mL/2fl oz cream (double)
1 tablespoon orange-flavoured liqueur

lamb
kebabs tuscany

ingredients

1½kg/3lb lean lamb, cut into 2½cm/1in cubes
1 green capsicum (pepper),
cut into 2½cm/1in cubes
1 red capsicum (pepper),
cut into 2½cm/1in cubes
2 onions, cut into eighths

Tuscan marinade:
½ cup tomato paste
½ cup oil
¼ cup red wine vinegar
3 cloves garlic, crushed
2 teaspoons oregano
½ teaspoon salt
pepper

Method:
1 *Combine marinade ingredients in a large bowl, mix well. Add lamb, capsicum and onion. Cover, leave at room temperature for at least 3 hours, or refrigerate overnight.*
2 *Thread alternate pieces of lamb, capsicum and onion onto skewers, cook on a lightly greased barbecue, basting and turning frequently, until meat is brown on the outside, still pink inside, about 12 minutes.*
Serves 8

oriental
beef spareribs

ingredients

2kg/4lb beef spareribs, all fat removed
Sambal Badjak*

Oriental Marinade:
½ cup light soy sauce
100ml/3fl oz freshly squeezed lemon juice
2 cloves garlic
3 tablespoons white wine vinegar
2 tablespoons dark brown sugar
2 tablespoons peanut oil
1 tablespoon grated fresh ginger
2 teaspoons ground coriander
½ teaspoon ground cumin
¼ teaspoon Tabasco sauce

Method:
1 *In a processor combine all marinade ingredients, puree until smooth. Place spareribs in a dish, pour over marinade, turn ribs to coat well. Cover and refrigerate overnight.*
2 *Remove ribs from marinade, barbecue until dark brown and crisp, turning once, about 6 minutes each side. Serve with Sambal Badjak for dipping.*
Note: *Sambal Badjak is available in Oriental foodstores*
Serves 8

Oven temperature 200°C/400°F/Gas 6

curried
sausage puffs

Method:

1 Cut pastry sheet in half

2 Combine mince, carrot, spring onion, chutney and curry powder, season to taste with salt and pepper, divide into 4, roll each into a sausage shape the length of the long side of the pastry.

3 Place sausage along pastry, roll up, and seal edge with water. Cut roll into 1cm/ $^1/_2$in slices.

4 Place slices onto greased baking trays, bake in moderately hot oven (200°C/400°F/Gas 6 for 15 minutes or until golden brown and puffed.

Makes 24

ingredients

2 sheet ready-rolled puff pastry
375g/$^3/_4$lb sausage mince
1 small carrot, finely grated
2 spring onions (scallions), chopped
1 tablespoon fruit chutney
1 teaspoon curry powder
salt
pepper

veal
and cherry with pepper sauce

Method:
1 *Combine marinade ingredients in a bowl. Add veal, toss well to coat, refrigerate overnight.*
2 *Thread alternate pieces o meat, tomato, capsicum and onion on skewers. Barbecue until meat is just cooked through.*
   Serves 8

ingredients

1kg/2 lb veal shoulder, trimmed of fat, cubed
16 cherry tomatoes
1 green capsicum(pepper), cubed
1 red capsicum (pepper), cubed
2 large onions, cut into eights

Onion marinade
1 onion, finely chopped
$1/2$ teaspoon cumin
1 teaspoon freshly squeezed lemon juice
$1/2$ teaspoon white wine vinegar
$1/4$ teaspoon chilli flakes
1 clove garlic, crushed

hot
capsicum (pepper) sauce

Method:
1 *Melt butter in a saucepan, add onion and capsicum. Saute until golden. Add tomatoes, chilli and water.*
2 *Bring to a boil, reduce heat, simmer 10 minutes. Season to taste with salt and freshly ground black pepper. Serve hot sprinkled with chopped coriander.*
   Makes about 1 cup

ingredients

1 tablespoon butter
1 onion, finely chopped
2 green capsicums (peppers), chopped
2 tomatoes, chopped
$1/4$ teaspoon chilli flakes
$1/3$ cup water
salt
pepper
1 tablespoon chopped coriander

oriental
chicken kebabs

Method:

1 Preheat barbecue to a high heat.
2 To make marinade, place sugar, lime leaves, if using, chilli, soy sauce and lime juice in a bowl and mix to combine.
3 Add chicken, toss to coat and marinate for 20 minutes. Drain chicken. Thread chicken and mushrooms onto lightly oiled skewers and cook on oiled barbecue grill, turning and basting with reserved marinade for 5 minutes or until chicken is tender and cooked.
4 Place snow pea (mangetout) sprouts or watercress, carrots and spring onions in a bowl. Combine sugar and lime juice, pour over salad and toss. Pile salad onto serving plates, then top with chicken kebabs.

Serves 6

ingredients

3 boneless chicken breast fillets, sliced
12 shiitake mushrooms
185g/6oz snow pea (mangetout) sprouts
or watercress
2 carrots, shredded
4 spring onions, chopped
2 teaspoons sugar
2 tablespoons lime juice

<u>Chilli and lime marinade</u>
1 tablespoon brown sugar
3 kaffir lime leaves, shredded (optional)
1 fresh red chilli, chopped
2 tablespoons soy sauce
1 tablespoon lime juice

Cooking is not an exact science: one does not require finely calibrated scales, pipettes and scientific equipment to cook, yet the conversion to metric measures in some countries and its interpretations must have intimidated many a good cook.

Weights are given in the recipes only for ingredients such as meats, fish, poultry and some vegetables. Though a few grams/ounces one way or another will not affect the success of your dish.

Though recipes have been tested using the Australian Standard 250mL cup, 20mL tablespoon and 5mL teaspoon, they will work just as well with the US and Canadian 8fl oz cup, or the UK 300mL cup. We have used graduated cup measures in preference to tablespoon measures so that proportions are always the same. Where tablespoon measures have been given, these are not crucial measures, so using the smaller tablespoon of the US or UK will not affect the recipe's success. At least we all agree on the teaspoon size.

For breads, cakes and pastries, the only area which might cause concern is where eggs are used, as proportions will then vary. If working with a 250mL or 300mL cup, use large eggs (60g/2oz), adding a little more liquid to the recipe for 300mL cup measures if it seems necessary. Use the medium-sized eggs (55g/1¹/₄oz) with 8fl oz cup measure. A graduated set of measuring cups and spoons is recommended, the cups in particular for measuring dry ingredients. Remember to level such ingredients to ensure their accuracy.

English measures

All measurements are similar to Australian with two exceptions: the English cup measures 300mL/ 10fl oz, whereas the Australian cup measure 250mL/8fl oz. The English tablespoon (the Australian dessertspoon) measures 14.8mL/¹/₂fl oz against the Australian tablespoon of 20mL/³/₄fl oz.

American measures

The American reputed pint is 16fl oz, a quart is equal to 32fl oz and the American gallon, 128fl oz. The Imperial measurement is 20fl oz to the pint, 40fl oz a quart and 160fl oz one gallon.

The American tablespoon is equal to 14.8mL/ ¹/₂fl oz, the teaspoon is 5mL/¹/₆fl oz. The cup measure is 250mL/8fl oz, the same as Australia.

Dry measures

All the measures are level, so when you have filled a cup or spoon, level it off with the edge of a knife. The scale below is the "cook's equivalent"; it is not an exact conversion of metric to imperial measurement. To calculate the exact metric equivalent yourself, use 2.2046 lb = 1kg or 1 lb = 0.45359kg

Metric		Imperial	
g = grams		oz = ounces	
kg = kilograms		lb = pound	
15g		¹/₂oz	
20g		²/₃oz	
30g		1oz	
60g		2oz	
90g		3oz	
125g		4oz	¹/₄ lb
155g		5oz	
185g		6oz	
220g		7oz	
250g		8oz	¹/₂ lb
280g		9oz	
315g		10oz	
345g		11oz	
375g		12oz	³/₄ lb
410g		13oz	
440g		14oz	
470g		15oz	
1,000g	1kg	35.2oz	2.2 lb
	1.5kg		3.3 lb

Oven temperatures

The Celsius temperatures given here are not exact; they have been rounded off and are given as a guide only. Follow the manufacturer's temperature guide, relating it to oven description given in the recipe. Remember gas ovens are hottest at the top, electric ovens at the bottom and convection-fan forced ovens are usually even throughout. We included Regulo numbers for gas cookers which may assist. To convert °C to °F multiply °C by 9 and divide by 5 then add 32.

Oven temperatures

	C°	F°	Regulo
Very slow	120	250	1
Slow	150	300	2
Moderately slow	150	325	3
Moderate	180	350	4
Moderately hot	190-200	370-400	5-6
Hot	210-220	410-440	6-7
Very hot	230	450	8
Super hot	250-290	475-500	9-10

Cake dish sizes

Metric	Imperial
15cm	6in
18cm	7in
20cm	8in
23cm	9in

Loaf dish sizes

Metric	Imperial
23x12cm	9x5in
25x8cm	10x3in
28x18cm	11x7in

Liquid measures

Metric	Imperial	Cup & Spoon
mL	fl oz	
millilitres	fluid ounce	
5mL	$1/6$fl oz	1 teaspoon
20mL	$2/3$fl oz	1 tablespoon
30mL	1fl oz	1 tablespoon plus 2 teaspoons
60mL	2fl oz	$1/4$ cup
85mL	$2^1/2$fl oz	$1/3$ cup
100mL	3fl oz	$3/8$ cup
125mL	4fl oz	$1/2$ cup
150mL	5fl oz	$1/4$ pint, 1 gill
250mL	8fl oz	1 cup
300mL	10fl oz	$1/2$ pint)
360mL	12fl oz	$1^1/2$ cups
420mL	14fl oz	$1^3/4$ cups
500mL	16fl oz	2 cups
600mL	20fl oz 1 pint,	$2^1/2$ cups
1 litre	35fl oz 1 $3/4$ pints,	4 cups

Cup measurements

One cup is equal to the following weights.

	Metric	Imperial
Almonds, flaked	90g	3oz
Almonds, slivered, ground	125g	4oz
Almonds, kernel	155g	5oz
Apples, dried, chopped	125g	4oz
Apricots, dried, chopped	190g	6oz
Breadcrumbs, packet	125g	4oz

	Metric	Imperial
Breadcrumbs, soft	60g	2oz
Cheese, grated	125g	4oz
Choc bits	155g	5oz
Coconut, desiccated	90g	3oz
Cornflakes	30g	1oz
Currants	155g	5oz
Flour	125g	4oz
Fruit, dried (mixed, sultanas etc)	185g	6oz
Ginger, crystallised, glace	250g	8oz
Honey, treacle, golden syrup	315g	10oz
Mixed peel	220g	7oz
Nuts, chopped	125g	4oz
Prunes, chopped	220g	7oz
Rice, cooked	155g	5oz
Rice, uncooked	220g	7oz
Rolled oats	90g	3oz
Sesame seeds	125g	4oz
Shortening (butter, margarine)	250g	8oz
Sugar, brown	155g	5oz
Sugar, granulated or caster	250g	8oz
Sugar, sifted icing	155g	5oz
Wheatgerm	60g	2oz

Length

Some of us still have trouble converting imperial length to metric. In this scale, measures have been rounded off to the easiest-to-use and most acceptable figures.

To obtain the exact metric equivalent in converting inches to centimetres, multiply inches by 2.54 whereby 1 inch equals 25.4 millimetres and 1 millimetre equals 0.03937 inches.

Metric	Imperial
mm=millimetres	in = inches
cm=centimetres	ft = feet
5mm, 0.5cm	$1/4$in
10mm, 1.0cm	$1/2$in
20mm, 2.0cm	$3/4$in
2.5cm	1in
5cm	2in
8cm	3in
10cm	4in
12cm	5in
15cm	6in
18cm	7in
20cm	8in
23cm	9in
25cm	10in
28cm	11in
30cm	1 ft, 12in

index